AN ENQUIRY

AN ENQUIRY

A MODERN EDITION OF A MISSIONS CLASSIC

William Carey

with Paige Patterson, Lea Eppling, and David Eppling

TMU PRESS
Truett McConnell University

Cleveland, Georgia

Copyright © 2021 by TMU Press

All rights reserved. No part of this book may be reproduced in any manner whatsoever without written permission except in the case of brief quotations embodied in critical articles and reviews.

First TMU Press Printing, 2021
Based on a reprint of the original 1792 version in 1818.

All Bible verses come from the King James Version translation.

Contents

Editorial Note	1
Foreword	5
Introduction	11
Section 1	15
Section 2	21
Section 3	41
Section 4	47
Section 5	55
Afterword	65
Addendum A: William Carey's Chart Analyzing World Population and Religious Belief at the End of the 18th Century	67
Contributors	83

Editorial Note

William Carey's *An Enquiry* has been republished several times since it first came out in 1792. Apparently, the first reprint appeared in 1818 while Carey was still actively stoking evangelistic flames in India. The second reproduction was the centennial edition, marking a hundred years since it first inspired an unprecedented global expansion of the church. Indeed, the year 1892 stood near the end of what the eminent church historian, Kenneth Scott Latourette, dubbed "The Great Century" of Christian missions. Furthermore, *An Enquiry* was republished at least three times in the 20th century (1934, 1961, and 1988).

TMU Press honors William Carey's legacy once again by republishing *An Enquiry*. Our editorial goal has been to offer this missions classic in a more reader-friendly style for modern readers. Hence, some of the archaic language, grammar, paragraph breaks, and spellings have been updated for clarity. Words in italics remain only where it seemed clear that emphasis in the original was intended by the author. Moreover, Carey's chart of global population and religious beliefs has been briefly summarized in the main body of the text while placing his detailed content in a separate addendum at the end. We believe this best fulfills our goal for modern readability without discrediting the painstaking statistical work Carey originally produced in 1792. The primary source for this edition of *An Enquiry* is the first reproduction in 1818.

TMU Press especially extends its appreciation to Christian author and editor, Lea Eppling, whose careful eye for grammatical detail remains a non-negotiable contribution for a literary project like this. She went beyond our expectations in assuring accuracy in many of the updates. Even so, any failures in this edition remain the sole property of TMU Press editors. Moreover, we also thank both Dr. Paige Patterson for his inspiring Foreword to this edition as well as David Eppling for the Afterword—a fitting conclusion rightly connecting Carey's heartbeat for global evangelism to the visionary heartbeat of Truett McConnell University and its president, Dr. Emir Caner, to take the gospel of Jesus Christ to the entire world for whom He died (John 3:16).

"From the very first verse to the very last tribe"

E. Peter Frank Lumpkins, PhD
Director of TMU Press
Associate Professor of Christian Studies
Truett McConnell University
100 Alumni Drive
Cleveland, GA 30528

For more information call 706.865.2134 or visit us on the web at www.truett.edu.

Foreword

Crocheted on the synapses of the mind of a 17-year-old teenager were the sounds and smells of Kolkata, where we had just landed on my first-ever jet airline flight in 1957, from the equally alluring scenes of Bangkok, Thailand. If Thailand were exotic, Kolkata was surreal. The cow that announced her arrival at my hotel room door with a guttural moo, snake charmers with cobras in the streets, Kolkata was the stuff of dreams for a teenaged youth. Then came the "hic-up drive," as I styled it out to Serampore, north of Kolkata, to the home of the storied missionary William Carey.

Before embarking on this 13-nation missionary journey, I had read a biography of Carey. Consequently, the sight of William Carey University was for me like taking in the Taj Mahal. Eventually we found ourselves in a large room exhibiting the history and the published works of William Carey. Carey, often referenced as the father of the modern missions movement, was certainly the quintessential missionary. Together with his associates John Clark Marshman, Joshua Marshman, and William Ward, Carey not only baptized a host of converts but also met the boat carrying Congregational missionaries Ann and Adoniram Judson, as well as Luther Rice, and baptized them, sending them on to Burma as Baptist missionaries.

Carey was a linguist par excellence. Knowledgeable in Latin, Greek, and Hebrew, he translated the entire Bible into Bengali, Sanskrit, Oriya, Marathi, Assamese, as well as parts of Scripture into more than twenty other languages. He also read French and Dutch, giving him the extended ability to work with the Kolkata merchants who employed these languages. He wrote dictionaries and grammars for some dialects that had no availability of such books and translated Hindu writings into English for use by missionaries.

Carey's work did not terminate at the church door. He was also a determined social reformer. Almost single-handedly, he opposed the practice of *suttee* (the burning of widows on the funeral pyres of their husbands) leading to its abolition in India. Observing the need for meaningful employment, Carey created an indigo factory that provided both labor and income for Indians. Carey also developed the Indian horticultural society and pioneered the development and use of drugs in India.

Additionally, Carey patiently endured hardship and suffering with stoic valor. A diminutive man, he nevertheless flexed his spiritual biceps in a fashion such that even enemies recognized him as God's man. He had to work under the intense opposition of the East India Company. In the process of this, Carey buried four of his children in Indian graves and was forced to stand by as the wife of his youth lost her mental hold on the world, declined, and died. Carey waited on her faithfully to the end.

Converted to non-conformist ideas quite early in his life, Carey joined a Particular Baptist church. He and Andrew Fuller, along with others, began to sense the call of God to go to the unevangelized masses in the pagan world. This in turn led to the 1792 publication of *An Enquiry into the Obligations of Christians to Use Means for the Conversion of the Heathens.* This short book insisting on human agency in taking the gospel message to those otherwise left in ignorance constituted the weapon used by God to explode the Calvinistic closed mind to human obligation to take the gospel to the earth's end. As such, this book remains forever a beacon and a monument. As a monument, the *Enquiry* remains a tribute to Carey, enshrining forever what it means to be a missionary. As a beacon, the penetrating beam of this lighthouse clarifies for all the mission task through the ages.

In 1988, under the perceptive missionary eye of Keith Eitel, the Criswell College republished *An Enquiry.* The text was edited by John Pretlove, also of the Criswell College faculty. Now once again in 2021, Truett McConnell University, out of the keen mission awareness of its president Emir Caner and its associate professor of history and Christian studies Peter Lumpkins, has grasped the importance of sustaining the influence of this volume. I thank God for William Carey, even as I thank the Lord for placing it in the hearts of Drs. Caner and Lumpkins to keep this before our students and in purview of the congregations of our churches.

Paige Patterson, President
Sandy Creek Foundation
2021

AN

ENQUIRY

INTO THE

OBLIGATIONS OF CHRISTIANS,

TO USE MEANS

FOR THE CONVERSION

OF

The Heathens;

In which the religious State of the different Nations of the World, the Success of former Undertakings, and the Practicability of further Undertakings, are considered.

—∞∞∞—

BY WILLIAM CAREY, D.D.

Professor of the Sungskritt, Mahratta, and Bengalee Languages, in the College of Fort William, and one of the Baptist Missionaries.

"For there is no difference between the Jew and the Greek; for the same Lord over all, is rich unto all that call upon him. For whosoever shall call on the name of the Lord, shall be saved. How then shall they call on him, in whom they have not believed? and how shall they believe in him of whom they have not heard? and how shall they hear without a Preacher? and how shall they preach except they be sent?" *Paul.*

LONDON:

PUBLISHED BY BUTTON AND SON, PATERNOSTER-ROW;
AND SOLD BY
T. INKERSLEY, BRADFORD; ROBINSON AND CO. AND G. WILSON,
LEEDS; HOLDEN, HALIFAX; COOMBE, LEICESTER; J. JAMES,
BRISTOL; AND ALL OTHER BOOKSELLERS.
1818.

Original title page (1818)

Introduction

As our blessed Lord has required us to pray that His kingdom may come, and His will be done on Earth as it is in Heaven, it becomes us not only to express our desires of that event by words, but to use every lawful method to spread the knowledge of that will. In order to do this, it is necessary that we become in some measure acquainted with the religious state of the world. As this is an object we should be prompted to pursue—not only by the gospel of our Redeemer, but even by the feelings of humanity—so an inclination to conscientious activity therein would form one of the strongest proofs that we are the subjects of grace, and partakers of that spirit of universal benevolence and genuine philanthropy, which appear so eminent in the character of God Himself.

Sin was introduced among the children of men by the fall of Adam, and has been spreading its baneful influence ever since. By changing its appearances to suit the circumstances of the times, it has grown up in ten thousand forms, and constantly counteracted the will and designs of God. One would have supposed that the remembrance of the deluge would have been communicated from father to son, and perpetually deterred mankind from transgressing the will of their Maker. But they were so blinded, that in the time of Abraham gross wickedness prevailed wherever colonies were planted, and the iniquity of the Amorites was great, though not yet full. After this, idolatry spread more and more, till the seven devoted nations were cut off with the most signal marks of divine displeasure. Still, however, the progress of evil was not stopped.

Too often, the Israelites themselves joined with the rest of mankind against the God of Israel. In one period the grossest ignorance and barbarism prevailed in the world. And afterwards, in a more enlightened age, the most daring infidelity and contempt of God; so that the world which was once overrun with ignorance, now "by wisdom knew not God" (1 Cor. 1:21), but "changed the glory of the uncorruptible God" as much as in the most barbarous ages, "into an image made like to corruptible man, and to birds, and four-footed beasts, and creeping things" (Rom. 1:23). Indeed, as they increased in science and politeness, they ran into more abundant and extravagant idolatries.

Yet God repeatedly made known His intention to prevail finally over all the power of the Devil, to destroy all his works, to set up His own kingdom and interest among men, and to extend it as universally as Satan had extended his. It was for this purpose that the Messiah came and died, that God might be just, and the Justifier of all that should believe in Him. When He had laid down His life, and taken it up again, He sent His disciples to preach the gospel to every creature, and to endeavor by all possible methods to bring over a lost world to God. They went according to their divine commission, and wonderful success attended their labors; the civilized Greeks and uncivilized Barbarians, each yielded to the Cross of Christ, embraced it as the only way of salvation.

Since the apostolic age many other attempts to spread the gospel have been made, which have been considerably successful. Yet, a very large proportion of mankind are still involved in all the darkness of heathenism. Some attempts are still in the making, but they are inconsiderable in comparison of what might be done if the whole body of Christians entered heartily into the spirit of the divine command on this subject. Some think little about it, others are unacquainted with the state of the world, and others love their wealth better than the souls of their fellow creatures.

In order that the subject may be taken into more serious consideration, I shall: 1) enquire whether the commission given by our Lord to His disciples is still binding on us, 2) take a short view of former undertakings, 3) give some account of the present state of the world, 4) consider the practicability of doing something more than is done, and 5) examine the duty of Christians in general in this matter.

Section 1

An enquiry as to whether the commission given by our Lord to His disciples is still binding on us.

Our Lord Jesus Christ, a little before His departure, commissioned His apostles to, "Go…and teach all nations" (Mat. 28:19); or, as another evangelist expresses it, "Go…into all the world, and preach the gospel to every creature" (Mark 16:15). This commission was as extensive as possible, and laid them under obligations to disperse themselves into every country of the habitable globe and preach to all the inhabitants of the world, without exception or limitation. They accordingly went forth in obedience to the command, and the power of God was clearly with them.

Many attempts of the same kind have been made since their day, which have been attended with various success; but the work has not been taken up or prosecuted of late years (except by a few individuals) with the zeal and perseverance with which the early Christians attempted it. It seems as if many thought the commission was sufficiently put in execution by what the apostles and others have done; that we have enough to do to attend to the salvation of our own countrymen; and that, if God intends the salvation of the heathen,

He will some way or other bring them to the gospel, or the gospel to them.

Therefore, multitudes sit at ease and give themselves no concern about the far greater part of their fellow sinners, who to this day are lost in ignorance and idolatry. There seems also to be an opinion existing in the minds of some, that because the apostles were extraordinary officers, and have no proper successors, and because many things which were right for them to do, would be utterly unwarrantable for us, therefore it may not be immediately binding on us to execute the commission, though it was so upon them. To the consideration of such people I would offer the following observations:

First, if the command of Christ to teach all nations is restricted to the apostles or those under the immediate inspiration of the Holy Ghost, then that of baptizing should be so too; and every denomination of Christians except the Quakers do wrong in baptizing with water at all.

Secondly, if the command of Christ to teach all nations is confined to the apostles, then all such ordinary ministers who have endeavored to carry the gospel to the heathens have acted without authorization, and run before they were sent. And though God has promised the most glorious things to the heathen world by sending His gospel to them; yet whoever goes first (or indeed at all) with that message, unless he has a new and special commission from Heaven, must go without any authority.

Thirdly, if the command of Christ to teach all nations extends only to the apostles, then, doubtless, the promise of the divine presence in this work must be so limited; but this is expressed in such a manner as entirely precludes such an idea. "Lo, I am with you always...to the end of the world" (Mat. 28:20).

That there are cases in which even a divine command may cease to be binding is admitted. As for instance, if it is *repealed*, as the ceremonial commandments of the Jewish law; or if there are no *subjects* in the world for the commanded act to be exercised upon, as in the law of septennial release, which might be dispensed with when there are no poor in the land to have their debts forgiven (Deut. 15:4). Or if, in any particular instance, we can produce a *counter revelation* of equal authority with the original command, as when Paul and Silas were forbidden of the Holy Ghost to preach the Word in Bithynia (Acts 16:6–7). Or if, in any case, there exists a *natural impossibility* of putting it in execution. It was not the duty of Paul to preach Christ to the inhabitants of Otaheite because no such place was then discovered, nor had he any means of coming at them. But none of these things can be alleged by us in behalf of the neglect of the commission given by Christ. We cannot say that it is repealed, like the commands of the ceremonial law; nor can we plead that there are no objects for the command to be exercised upon.

Sadly, the far greater part of the world, as we shall see presently, is still covered with heathen darkness! Nor can we produce a counter revelation concerning any particular nation, like that to Paul and Silas concerning Bithynia; and if we could, it would not warrant our sitting still and neglecting all the other parts of the world; for Paul and Silas, when forbidden to preach to those heathens, went elsewhere and preached to others. Neither can we allege a natural impossibility in the case. It has been said that we ought not to force our way, but to wait for the openings and leadings of Providence; but it might be answered with equal propriety in this case, neither ought we to neglect to embrace those openings in providence which daily present themselves to us. What openings in providence do we wait for? We can neither expect to be transported into the heathen world without ordinary means, nor to be endowed with the gift of tongues when we arrive there. These would not be providential interpositions, but miraculous ones. Where a command exists, nothing can be necessary to render it binding but a removal of those obstacles which render obedience impossible, and these are removed already. Natural impossibility can never be pleaded, so long as facts exist to prove the contrary.

Have not the Catholic missionaries surmounted all those difficulties which we have generally thought to be insuperable? Have not the missionaries of the *Unitas Fratrum*, or Moravian Brethren, encountered the scorching heat of Abyssinia, and the frozen climes of Greenland and Labrador along with their difficult languages and savage manners? Or have not English traders, for the sake of gain, surmounted all those things which have generally been counted insurmountable obstacles in the way of preaching the gospel? Witness the trade to Persia, the East Indies, China, and Greenland; even the accursed slave trade on the coasts of Africa. Men can insinuate themselves into the favor of the most barbarous clans and uncultivated tribes for the sake of gain; and however different the circumstances of trading and preaching are, yet this will prove the possibility of ministers being introduced there; and if this is but thought a sufficient reason to make the experiment, my point is gained.

It has been said that some learned Bible interpreters have proved from Scripture that the time is not yet come that the heathen should be converted; and that first the "two witnesses" must be slain (Rev. 11:3–7), and many other prophecies fulfilled. But admitting this to be the case (which I much doubt[1]), if any objection is made from this against preaching to them immediately, it must be founded on one of these things; either that the secret purpose of God is the rule of our duty, and then it must be as improper to pray for them as to preach to them; or else that none shall be converted in the heathen world till the universal outpouring of the Spirit in the last days. But this objection comes too late; for the success of the gospel has been very considerable in many places already.

It has been objected that there are multitudes in our own nation, and within our immediate spheres of action, who are as ignorant as the South Sea savages, and that therefore we have work enough at home without going into other countries. That there are thousands in our own land as far from God as possible, I readily grant, and that this ought to excite us to tenfold diligence in our work, and in attempts to spread divine knowledge among them, is a certain fact; but that it ought to supersede all attempts to spread the gospel in foreign parts, seems to want proof. Our own countrymen have the means of grace, and may attend on the Word preached if they choose. They have the means of knowing the truth, and faithful ministers are placed in almost every part of the land, whose spheres of action might be much extended, if their congregations were heartier and more active in the cause. But the case is widely different with the heathen, who have no Bible, no written language (which many of them have not), no ministers, no good civil government, nor any of those advantages which we have.

Therefore, pity, humanity, and much more Christianity, call loudly for every possible exertion to introduce the gospel among them.

Section 2

Containing a short review of former undertakings for the conversion of the heathen.

Before the coming of our Lord Jesus Christ the whole world were either heathens or Jews; and both, as to the body of them, were enemies to the gospel. After the resurrection the disciples continued in Jerusalem till Pentecost. Being daily engaged in prayer and supplication, and having chosen Matthias to supply the place of Judas in the apostolic office, on that solemn day, when they were all assembled together, a most remarkable effusion of the Holy Spirit took place and a capacity of speaking in all foreign languages was bestowed upon them. This opportunity was embraced by Peter for preaching the gospel to a great congregation of Jews and proselytes, who were from Parthia, Media, Elam, Mesopotamia, Judea, Cappadocia, the proconsular Asia, Phrygia, Pamphylia, Egypt, Lybia, Crete, Arabia, and Rome, etc. At the first effort, God worked so powerfully that three thousand were converted, who immediately after were baptized and added to the church (Acts 2). Before this great addition they consisted of "about an hundred and twenty" people (Acts 1:15), but from that time they continually increased.

It was but a little after this that Peter and John, going up to the temple, healed the lame man. This miracle drew a great multitude together, and while they stood wondering at the event Peter took occasion to preach Jesus Christ to them. As a result, five thousand more believed (Acts 3:1–4:4). This was not done without opposition; the priests and Sadducees tried all the methods they could devise to prevent them from preaching the gospel. The apostles, however, asserted their divine warrant, and as soon as they were set at liberty addressed God, and prayed that a divine power might attend their labors. Their petition was heard and their future ministry was very successful. On account of the needs of those engaged in this good work, those among them who had possessions or goods, sold them and devoted the money to virtuous uses.

About this time, a man and his wife—acting with great pretensions to piety—sold an estate and brought part of the money to the apostles, pretending it to be the whole; for which dissimulation both he and his wife were struck dead by the hand of God. This awful catastrophe, however, was the occasion of many more men and women being added to the church. The miracles performed by the apostles, and the success attending their ministry, stirred up greater envy in the priests and Sadducees, who imprisoned them; from which confinement they were soon liberated by an angel; upon which, they went immediately as they were commanded and preached in the temple. Here they were seized and brought before the council, where Gamaliel spoke in their favor, and they were dismissed (Acts 5). After this, they continued their work, rejoicing that they were counted worthy to suffer shame for the name of Christ.

By this time, the church at Jerusalem was so increased that the multiplicity of its temporal concerns was the occasion of some neglects, which produced a dissatisfaction. The apostles, therefore, recommended to the church to choose seven devout men, whose office it should be to attend upon its temporal affairs; that they might give themselves to "prayer, and to the ministry of the word" (Acts 6:4). Seven were accordingly chosen, over whom the apostles prayed, and ordained them to the office of deacons by the laying on of hands. These things being settled, the church increased more and more (Acts 6:7). One of these deacons, whose name was Stephen, being a person of eminent knowledge and holiness, performed many miracles, and disputed with great evidence and energy for the truth of Christianity, which raised up a number of opponents. These soon procured his death, and carried their resentment so far as to stir up such a persecution that the church, which till now had been confined to Jerusalem, was dispersed, and all the preachers except the apostles were driven from that place, and went everywhere preaching the Word (Acts 7:1–8:4).

A young man named Saul was very active in this persecution. He had been educated under Gamaliel (a member of the Sanhedrin), was a person of promising genius, a Pharisee by profession, and much attached to the Jewish ceremonies. When Stephen was stoned, Saul appeared much pleased with it, and had custody of the clothes of his executioners; and from that time, was fired with such a spirit of persecution himself, that he went about dragging some to prison, and compelling others to blaspheme the name of the Lord Jesus.

Neither was he contented with exercising his rage at Jerusalem, but went to the chief priests and obtained testimonials of authority to carry on the same work at Damascus. But on his way, as he was almost ready to enter into the city, the Lord changed his heart in a very wonderful manner; so that instead of entering the city to persecute, he began to preach the gospel as soon as he was able. This presently brought upon him the same persecution which he had designed to employ on others, and even endangered his life, so that the brethren found it necessary to let him down from the city wall in a basket by night; and so he escaped the hands of his enemies. From there he went to Jerusalem where he preached the Word, but being persecuted he went to Caesarea, and from there to Tarsus (Acts 9).

In the time of this trouble in the church, Philip went and preached in Samaria with great success. So great was the work that an impostor, who had deceived the people with sleight of hand and trickery for a long time, was so amazed and even convinced, as to profess himself a Christian and was baptized; but was afterwards detected, and appeared to be a hypocrite. Besides him a great number believed in reality; and being baptized, a church was formed there. Soon after this the Lord commanded Philip to go the way which led from Jerusalem to Gaza, which he did, and there found a Eunuch of great authority in the court of Ethiopia, to whom he preached Christ. The Eunuch believed and was baptized; after which Philip preached at Ashdod, or Azotus (Acts 8:5–40).

About the same time Peter went to Lydda, or Diospolis,

and cured Aeneas of a palsy, which was the means of the conversion not only of the inhabitants of that town, but also of the neighboring country, called Saron, the capital of which was Lasharon. While he was there, a circumstance presented itself which tended much to the spread of the truth. A woman of Joppa (a seaport town in the neighborhood) died, so they sent to Lydda for Peter, who went over, and when he had prayed, she was raised to life again; which was an occasion of the conversion of many in that town. Peter continued preaching there for some time and lodged at the house of a tanner (Acts 9:32–43).

Another circumstance also tended to the further propagation of Christianity. A Roman military officer who had some acquaintance with the Old Testament Scriptures, but was not circumcised, was one day engaged in prayer in his house at Caesarea, when an angel appeared to him and bid him send for Peter from Joppa to preach in his house. Before this time, the work of God had been wholly confined to the Jews and Jewish proselytes. Even the apostles appeared to have had very contracted ideas of the Christian dispensation; but now God by a vision revealed to Peter that Christianity was to be spread into all nations. Accordingly, he went and preached in the house of Cornelius at Caesarea, where several were converted and baptized, and the foundation of a church was laid in that city (Acts 10). Some of the dispersed ministers, having fled to Antioch in Syria, began to preach to the Greeks in that city about the same time, and had good success; upon which the apostles sent Paul and Barnabas, who instructed and strengthened them, and a church was formed in that city also, which in a little time sent out several eminent preachers (Acts 11:19–26).

In the Acts of the Apostles we have an account of four of the principal journeys which Paul and his companions undertook. The first, in which he was accompanied by Barnabas, is recorded in the thirteenth and fourteenth chapters, and was the first *attack* on the heathen world. It was a journey into Asia Minor. On their way, they passed over the island of Cyprus. No sooner had they entered on their undertaking than they met with great difficulty; for Mark, whom they had taken as their minister, deserted them and returned to Jerusalem, where, it seems, he thought he should enjoy the greatest quiet. Paul and Barnabas, however, went forward. In every city they preached the Word of the Lord, entering into the Jewish synagogues, first preaching Christ to them, and then to the Gentiles. They were heard with great candor and eagerness by some, and rejected by others with obstinacy, wrath, and cruel persecution. Once, it was all they could do to restrain the people from worshiping them as gods. Soon after, Paul was stoned, dragged out of the city, and left for dead.

Having penetrated as far as Derbe, they thought it proper to return by the way that they came, calling at every city where they had sown the good seed. In most, if not all these places, some had embraced the gospel. They exhorted and strengthened them in the faith, formed them into churches and ordained them elders, and fasted and prayed with them. So having commended them to the Lord on whom they had believed, Paul and Barnabas returned to Antioch in Syria, from where they first set out, reporting to the church all that

God had done by them, and how He had opened the door of faith to the Gentiles.

About this time, a dispute arose in the churches concerning circumcision. Paul and Barnabas were chosen to go up to Jerusalem to consult the apostles and elders on the subject. This business being concluded, they (accompanied with Judas and Silas), returned to Antioch with the general resolution, and continued there for a season, teaching and preaching the Word of the Lord (Acts 15:1–35).

Paul now proposed to Barnabas, his fellow laborer, that they might visit their brethren in the places where they had been already, and see how they did. To this Barnabas readily agreed; but a difference arose between them about taking John Mark, who had deserted them before. So these two eminent servants of God parted, and never appear to have traveled together anymore. They continued, however, each to serve in the cause of Christ, though they could not walk together.

Barnabas took John, and sailed to Cyprus, his native island. Paul took Silas, and went through Syria and Cilicia, to Derbe and Lystra—cities where he and Barnabas had preached in their first excursion (Acts 15:36–41). Here they found Timothy, a promising young man, whom they encouraged to engage in the ministry.

Paul being now at Lystra, which was the boundary of his first excursion, and having visited the churches already planted, and delivered to them the decrees of the apostles and elders relating to circumcision, seems to have felt his heart enlarged, and endeavored to carry on the glorious work of preaching the gospel to the heathen to a greater extent. With

Silas and Timothy, his second journey[2] took a western direction, passing through Phrygia and the region of Galatia. Having preached the Word in these parts with considerable success,[3] he and his companions wished to have gone into the proconsular Asia, and afterward tried to go into Bithynia; but were forbidden of the Holy Ghost, who seems to have had a special design of employing them elsewhere.

Passing by Mysia, they came down to Troas on the seacoast. Here a vision appeared to Paul, in which he was invited to go over to Macedonia. Obedient to the heavenly vision, and greatly encouraged by it, they crossed the Aegean Sea with all speed, and passing through the island of Samothracia, landed at Neapolis, and went from there to Philippi, the chief city of that part of Macedonia. It was here that Paul preached on a Sabbath day to a few women by a riverside, and Lydia (a woman of Thyatira) was converted and baptized, and her household with her. It was here that a poor girl, who brought her employers considerable profit by foretelling future events, followed the apostles and had her spirit of divination ejected; on which account her masters were much irritated, and raised a tumult, the effect of which was that Paul and Silas were imprisoned. But even this was overruled for the success of the gospel, in that the keeper of the prison, and all his house, were thereby brought to believe in the Lord Jesus Christ and were baptized (Acts 16).

From Philippi they passed through Amphipolis, Apollonia, Thessalonica (now Salonica), Berea, Athens, and Corinth—preaching the gospel wherever they went. From there Paul took a ship and sailed to Syria, only giving a short call at Ephesus, determining to be at Jerusalem at the feast of the Passover. Having greeted the church, he came to Caesarea, and went from there to Antioch (Acts 17:1–18:22).

Here ended Paul's second journey, which was very extensive, taking several years. He and his companions met with their difficulties in it, but likewise had their encouragements. They were persecuted at Philippi, as already noticed, and generally found the Jews to be their most adamant enemies. These would raise tumults, inflame the minds of the Gentiles against them, and follow them from place to place—doing all the mischief in their power. This was the case especially at Thessalonica, Berea, and Corinth. But amidst all their persecutions, God was with them and strengthened them in various ways.

At Berea, they were openly received, and their doctrine fairly tried by the Holy Scriptures. "Therefore," it is said, "many of them believed" (Acts 17:12). At other places, the Jews tried to influence people to despise the apostle, yet some welcomed and embraced him. At Corinth, opposition rose to a great height, but the Lord appeared to His servant in a vision, saying, "Be not afraid, but speak, and hold not thy peace: For I am with thee, and no man shall set on thee to hurt thee: for I have much people in this city" (Acts 18:9–10). And the promise was made abundantly good in the spirit exhibited by Gallio, the proconsul, who turned a deaf ear to the accusations of the Jews, and nobly declined interfering in matters beside his province. Upon the whole, a number of churches were planted during this journey, which for ages after shone as lights in the world.

When Paul had visited Antioch and spent some time there, he prepared for a third journey into heathen countries;

the account of which is found in Acts 18:23–21:17. At his first setting out he went over the whole country of Galatia and Phrygia in order, strengthening all the disciples; and passing through the upper coasts came to Ephesus. There, for the space of three months, he boldly preached in the Jewish synagogue, disputing, and persuading the things concerning the kingdom of God.

But when the hardened Jews openly rejected the gospel, and spoke evil of that way before the multitude, Paul openly separated the disciples from them and assembled in the school of one Tyrannus. "This," it is said, "continued by the space of two years; so that all they which dwelt in the proconsular Asia heard the Word of the Lord Jesus, both Jews and Greeks" (Acts 19:10). About this time, certain magicians were exposed and others converted, who burnt their books and confessed their deeds. So mightily grew the Word of the Lord, and prevailed.

After this, an uproar having been raised by Demetrius the silversmith, Paul went into Macedonia, visited the churches planted in his former journey, and from there passed into Greece. Having preached in different places for three months, he thought of sailing directly to Syria; but in order to avoid the Jews who laid wait for him near the seacoast, he took another course through Macedonia, and from there to Troas, by the way of Philippi. There is no mention made in his former journey of his having preached at Troas; yet it seems he did, and a church was gathered, with whom the apostle at this time united in "breaking of bread" (Acts 20:7). It was here that he preached all night and raised Eutychus, who being overcome with sleep had fallen down and was taken up dead.

From here, they sailed for Syria, and in their way called at Miletus, where Paul sent for the elders of the church of Ephesus, and delivered that most solemn and affectionate farewell, recorded in the twentieth chapter of the Acts of the Apostles. From here, they sailed for Tyre, where they tarried seven days, and from there proceeded to Jerusalem.

Paul's fourth and last journey (or rather voyage) was to Rome, where he went as a prisoner. For while at Jerusalem he was quickly apprehended by the Jews; but being rescued by Lysias, the chief captain, he was sent to Caesarea to take his trial. Here he made his defense before Felix and Drusilla in such a way that the judge, instead of the prisoner, was made to tremble. Here also he made his defense before Festus, Agrippa, and Bernice—with such force of evidence that Agrippa was almost persuaded to be a Christian.

But the malice of the Jews being insatiable, and Paul finding himself in danger of being delivered into their hands, was constrained to appeal unto Caesar. This was the occasion of his being sent to Rome, where he arrived after a long and dangerous voyage. While shipwrecked on the island of Melita, Paul performed miracles, and Publius, the governor, was converted (Acts 27:17–28:10).

When Paul arrived at Rome he addressed his countrymen, the Jews, some of whom believed. But when others rejected the gospel, he turned from them to the Gentiles. For two whole years Paul dwelt in his own hired house, preaching the kingdom of God and teaching those things which concerned the Lord Jesus Christ, with all confidence; no man forbidding him (Acts 28:16–31).

Thus far the history of the Acts of the Apostles informs

us of the success of the Word in the early days of the church; and history informs us of its being preached about this time in many other places. Peter speaks of a church at Babylon (1 Pet. 5:13); Paul proposed a journey to Spain (Rom.15:24), and it is generally believed he went there, and likewise came to France and Britain. Andrew preached to the Scythians, north of the Black Sea. John is said to have preached in India, and we know that he was at the Isle of Patmos, in the Archipelago. Philip is reported to have preached in upper Asia, Scythia, and Phrygia; Bartholomew in India, on this side the Ganges, Phrygia, and Armenia; Matthew in Arabia, or Asiatic Ethiopia, and Parthia; Thomas in India, as far as the coast of Coromandel, and some say in the island of Ceylon; Simon the Canaanite (also known as Simon the Zealot) in Egypt, Cyrene, Mauritania, Lybia, and other parts of Africa, and from there to have come to Britain; and Jude is said to have been principally engaged in Asia Minor and Greece.

Their labors were evidently very extensive, and very successful; so that Pliny the Younger (who lived soon after the death of the apostles) in a letter to the emperor Trajan, observed that Christianity had spread not only through towns and cities but also through whole countries. Indeed before this, in the time of Nero, it was so prevalent that it was opposed by an imperial edict. Accordingly, the proconsuls and other governors were commissioned to destroy it.

Justin Martyr (who lived about the middle of the second century) observed in his dialogue with Trypho that there was no part of mankind—whether Greeks or barbarians, or any others, by whatsoever name they are called, whether Samaritans, or nomads who had no houses, or the Scenites of Arabia

Petraea who lived in tents among their cattle—where supplications and thanksgivings are not offered up to the Father and Maker of all things, through the name of Jesus Christ.

Irenaeus (who lived about the year 170) speaks of churches that were founded in Germany, Spain, France, the eastern countries, Egypt, Lybia, and the middle of the world. Tertullian (who lived and wrote at Carthage in Africa about twenty years afterwards), enumerating the countries where Christianity had penetrated, makes mention of the Parthians, Medes, Elamites, Mesopotamians, Armenians, Phrygians, Cappadocians, the inhabitants of Pontus, Asia, Pamphylia, Egypt and the regions of Africa beyond Cyrene, the Romans and Jews (formerly of Jerusalem), many of the Gaetuli, many borders of the Mauri (or Moors) in Mauritania (now Barbary), Morocco, etc., all the borders of Spain, many nations of the Gauls, and the places in Britain which were inaccessible to the Romans; the Dacians, Sarmatians, Germans, Scythians. Added to these are the inhabitants of many hidden nations, provinces, and islands which he could not enumerate because they were unknown to him.

The labors of the ministers of the gospel in this early period were so remarkably blessed of God that the last mentioned writer observed in a letter to Scapula that if he began a persecution, the city of Carthage would be decimated. So abundant were they in the three first centuries, that ten years of constant and almost universal persecution under Diocletian could neither root out the Christians nor prejudice their cause.

After this they had great encouragement under several emperors, particularly Constantine and Theodosius, and a very great work of God was carried on. But the ease and affluence which attended the church in these times served to introduce a flood of corruption, which by degrees brought on the whole system of popery, by means of which all appeared to be lost again. Satan set up his kingdom of darkness, deceit, and human authority over conscience through all the Christian world.

In the time of Constantine, one Frumentius was sent to preach to the Indians, and met with great success. A young woman who was a Christian, being taken captive by the Iberians, or Georgians, near the Caspian Sea, informed them of the truths of Christianity, and was so much regarded that they sent to Constantine for ministers to come and preach the Word to them.

About the same time some barbarous nations, having made irruptions into Thrace, carried away several Christians captive who preached the gospel; by which means the inhabitants upon the Rhine, and the Danube, the Celtae, and some other parts of Gaul, were brought to embrace Christianity. Also about this time, James of Nisbis went into Persia to strengthen the Christians and preach to the heathens. His success was so great that Adiabene was almost entirely Christian.

About the year 372, a monk named Moses went to preach to the Saracens (who then lived in Arabia), where he had great success. At this time the Goths and other northern nations had the kingdom of Christ further extended among them, but were very soon corrupted with Arianism.

Soon after this the kingdom of Christ was further extended among the Scythian nomads beyond the Danube; and about the year 430, a people called the Burgundians received the gospel. Four years after that Palladius was sent to preach in Scotland. The next year, Patrick was sent from Scotland to preach to the Irish; who before his time were totally uncivilized and, some say, cannibals. He, however, was useful and laid the foundations of several churches in Ireland.

Shortly after this, truth spread further among the Saracens, and in 522 Zathus king of the Colchians encouraged it, and many of that nation were converted to Christianity. About this time also, the work was extended in Ireland by Finian, and in Scotland by Constantine and Columba; the latter of whom, preached also to the Picts. Brudaeus, their king, was converted along with several others. About 541, Adad, the king of Ethiopia, was converted by the preaching of Mansionarius; the Heruli beyond the Danube were now made obedient to the faith, as were the Abasgi near the Caucasian Mountains.

But now Roman Catholicism, especially the compulsive part of it, was risen to such a height that the usual method of propagating the gospel, or rather what was so called, was to conquer pagan nations by force of arms, and then oblige them to submit to Christianity; after which bishoprics were erected and people were sent to instruct the people. I shall just mention some of those who are said to have labored in this manner.

In 596, Austin the monk, Melitus, Justus, Paulinus, and Ruffinian labored in England, and in their way were very successful. Paulinus, who appears to have been one of the best of them, had great success in Northumberland; Birinus preached to the West Saxons, and Felix to the East Angles.

In 589 Amandus Gallus labored in Ghent, Chelenus in Artois, and Gallus and Columbanus in Suabia. In 648, Egidius Gallus in Flanders, and the two Evaldi in Westphalia. In 684, Willifred in the Isle of Wight. In 688, Chilianus in upper Franconia. In 698, Boniface, or Winifred, among the Thuringians near Erford in Saxony, and Willibroad in West-Friesland. Charlemagne conquered Hungary in the year 800, and obliged the inhabitants to profess Christianity, when Modestus likewise preached to the Venedi at the source of the Save and Drave. In 833 Ansgarius preached in Denmark, Gaudibert in Sweden, and about 861, Methodius and Cyril in Bohemia.

About the year 500, the Scythians overran Bulgaria, and Christianity was wiped out; but about 870, they were reconverted. Poland began to be brought over about the same time, and afterwards—about 960 or 990—the work was further extended amongst the Poles and Prussians. The work was begun in Norway in 960, and in Muscovy in 989, the Swedes propagated Christianity in Finland in 1168, Lithuania became Christian in 1386, and Samogitia in 1439. The Spaniards forced Roman Catholicism upon the inhabitants of South America, as did the Portuguese in Asia. The Jesuits were sent into China in 1552. Xavier, whom they called the apostle of the Indians, labored in the East Indies and Japan from 1541 to 1552, and several missions of Capauchins were sent to Africa in the seventeenth century. But blind zeal, gross superstition, and infamous cruelties, so marked the appearances of religion all this time that the professors of Christianity needed conversion as much as the heathen world.

A few devout and virtuous people had fled from the general corruption, and lived obscurely in the valleys of Piedmont and Savoy. They were like the seed of the church. Some of them, now and then, needed to travel into other parts, where they faithfully testified against the corruptions of the times. About 1369, Wickliffe began to preach the faith in England. His preaching and writings were the means of the conversion of great numbers, many of whom became excellent preachers. A work was begun, which afterwards spread in England, Hungary, Bohemia, Germany, Switzerland, and many other places. John Huss and Jerome of Prague preached boldly and successfully in Bohemia and the adjacent parts. In the following century Luther, Calvin, Melancthon, Bucer, Martyr, and many others stood up against all the rest of the world; they preached, and prayed, and wrote; and nations agreed one after another to cast off the yoke of Roman Catholicism, and to embrace the doctrine of the gospel.

In England, episcopal tyranny replaced Roman Catholic cruelty, which in the year 1620 obliged many devout people to leave their native land and settle in America. These were followed by others in 1629, who laid the foundations of several gospel churches which have increased amazingly since that time, and the Redeemer has fixed His throne in that country where but a little time ago Satan had universal dominion.

In 1632 Mr. Elliot of New England, a very devout and zealous minister, began to preach to the Indians, among whom he had great success. Several churches of Indians were planted, and some preachers and schoolmasters raised up among them; since which time others have labored among them with some good encouragement. About the year 1743,

Mr. David Brainerd was sent as a missionary to some more Indians, where he preached and prayed; and after some time an extraordinary work of conversion took place, and wonderful success attended his ministry. And at this present time, Mr. Kirkland and Mr. Sergeant are employed in the same good work, and God has considerably blessed their labors.

In 1706 the king of Denmark sent a Mr. Ziegenbalg and some others to Tranquebar on the Coromandel coast in the East Indies. They were useful to the natives, so that many of the heathens were turned to the Lord.

Likewise, the Dutch East India Company, having extended their commerce, built the city of Batavia, and a church was opened there. The Lord's Supper was administered for the first time on January 3, 1621 by their minister, James Hulzibos. Hereafter, some ministers were sent to Amboyna, who were very successful. A seminary of learning was erected at Leyden, in which ministers and assistants were educated under the renowned Walaeus.

For some years a great number were sent to the East, at the Company's expense, so that in a little time many thousands at Formoso, Malabar, Ternate, Jaffanapatnam, in the town of Columba, at Amboyna, Java, Banda, and Macassar embraced the religion of our Lord Jesus Christ. The work has decayed in some places, but they now have churches in Ceylon, Sumatra, Java, Amboyna, and some other of the spice islands, and at the Cape of Good Hope in Africa.

But none of the moderns have equaled the Moravian Brethren in this good work. They have sent missions to Greenland, Labrador, and several of the West Indies' islands, which have been blessed for good. They have likewise sent to

Abyssinia in Africa, but what success they have had I cannot tell.

The late Mr. Wesley made an effort in the West Indies, and some of their ministers are now laboring among the Caribs and Negroes, and I have seen pleasing accounts of their success.

Section 3

Containing a survey of the present state of the world.

In this survey I shall consider the world as divided into four parts, according to its usual division—Europe, Asia, Africa, and the Americas; and take notice of the extent of the several countries, their population, civilization, and religion. The article of religion I shall divide into Christian, Jewish, Muslim, and pagan; and shall now and then hint at the particular sect of them that prevails in the places described. The following will exhibit a more comprehensive view of what I propose than any words I can offer on the subject.

[*Editor's note: What follows here in the original version is an extended chart Carey composed of the known world at the time, a chart somewhat confusing to the modern reader. Rather than duplicate the chart here, the editors chose to summarize Carey's research and post the full content of his chart in an appendix at the book's end. We trust this decision does not obscure or skew Carey's original intent*].

Division	Europe	Asia	Africa	Americas
Estimated Inhabitants	166,174,000	399,265,500	61,137,200	117,056,420
Religious Beliefs	Christianity (mostly Catholic and Protestant), Muslims and some Pagans	Mostly Muslims and Pagans; smaller number of Christians	Christian (mostly Catholic), Pagan, and Muslims	Mostly Christian (both Catholic and Protestant) and Pagans

This, as nearly as I can obtain information, is the state of the world; though in many countries such as Turkey, Arabia, Great Tartary, Africa, and America except the United States, and most of the Asiatic Islands, we have no accounts of the number of inhabitants that can be relied on. Therefore, I have only calculated the extent, and counted a certain number on an average per square mile; in some countries more, and in others less, according as circumstances determine. A few general remarks will conclude this section.

First, the inhabitants of the world according to this calculation amount to about seven hundred and thirty-one million; four hundred and twenty million of whom are still in pagan darkness; one hundred and thirty million are followers of Muhammad; one hundred million are Catholics; forty-four million are Protestants; thirty million are of the Greek Orthodox and Armenian churches; and perhaps seven million are Jews. It must undoubtedly strike every contemplative mind that a vast proportion of the sons of Adam remain in the most deplorable state of heathen darkness, without any means of knowing the true God, except what is given through the works of nature; and utterly destitute of the knowledge of the gospel of Christ, or of any means of obtaining it.

Many of these countries have no written language, and consequently no Bible. They are led only by the most childish customs and traditions. Such, for instance, are all the middle and back parts of North America, the inland parts of South America, the South Sea Islands, New Holland, New Zealand, New Guinea; and I may add Great Tartary, Siberia, Samojedia, and the other parts of Asia contiguous to the frozen sea; the greatest part of Africa, the island of Madagascar, and many places beside.

In many of these parts they are also cannibals, feeding upon the flesh of their slain enemies with the greatest brutality and eagerness. The truth of this was ascertained beyond a doubt, by the late eminent navigator, Cooke, regarding the New Zealanders and some of the inhabitants of the western coast of America. Human sacrifices are also very frequently offered. So much so that scarcely a week goes by without instances of this kind. They are in general poor, barbarous, naked pagans, as destitute of civilization, as they are of true religion.

Secondly, barbarous as these poor heathens are, they appear to be as capable of knowledge as we are; and in many places, at least, have demonstrated uncommon genius and teachability. I greatly question whether most of the barbarities practiced by them have not originated in some real or supposed affront; and might therefore be better understood as acts of self-defense than proofs of inhuman and bloodthirsty dispositions.

Thirdly, in other parts where they have a written language, as in the East Indies, China, Japan, etc., they know nothing of the gospel. The Jesuits indeed once made many converts to popery among the Chinese; but their highest aim seemed to be to obtain their good opinion. For even though the converts professed themselves Christians, they still honored the image of Confucius, their great lawgiver. Their ambitious intrigues eventually brought the displeasure of the government upon them, which resulted in the suppression of the mission, and almost, if not entirely, of the Christian name. It is also a melancholy fact that the vices of Europeans have been communicated wherever they themselves have been; so that the religious state of even heathens has been rendered worse by interaction with them!

Fourthly, a very great proportion of Asia and Africa (along with some part of Europe) are Muslims. Those in Persia who are of the sect of Hali, are the most inveterate enemies to the Turks; and they in return abhor the Persians. The Africans are some of the most ignorant of all the Muslims; especially the Arabs, who are scattered through all the northern parts of Africa and who live by continually plundering their neighbors.

Fifthly, in respect to those who bear the Christian name, a very great degree of ignorance and immorality abounds among them. There are Christians (or at least so called) of the Greek Orthodox and Armenian churches in all the Muslim countries; but they are, if possible, more ignorant and vicious than the Muslims themselves. The Georgian Christians, who are near the Caspian Sea, maintain themselves by selling their neighbors, relatives, and children as slaves to the Turks and Persians. And it is remarked that if any of the Greek Orthodox of Anatolia turn Muslim, the Turks never think very highly of them, on account of their being known for dishonesty and hypocrisy. It is well known that most of the members of the Greek Orthodox Church are very ignorant.

Roman Catholics are also generally ignorant of divine things and very vicious. Nor do the bulk of the Church of England much exceed them—either in knowledge or holiness. Many errors, and much looseness of conduct, are found among dissenters of all denominations. The Lutherans in Denmark are much on par with the Church of England. The face of most Christian countries presents a dreadful scene of ignorance, hypocrisy, and extravagance. Various baneful and pernicious errors appear to gain ground in almost every part of Christendom. The truths of the gospel, and even the gospel itself, are attacked, and every method that the enemy can invent is employed to undermine the kingdom of our Lord Jesus Christ.

All these things are loud calls to Christians, and especially to ministers, to exert themselves to the utmost in their several spheres of action, and to try to enlarge them as much as possible.

Section 4

The practicability of something being done, more than what is done, for the conversion of the heathen.

The impediments in the way of carrying the gospel among the heathen must arise, I think, from one or other of the following things: their distance from us, their barbarous and savage manner of living, the danger of being killed by them, the difficulty of procuring the necessities of life, or the unintelligibleness of their languages.

First—their distance from us. Whatever objections might have been made on that account before the invention of the mariner's compass, nothing can be alleged for it, with any color of plausibility in the present age. Men can now sail with as much certainty through the Great South Sea, as they can through the Mediterranean, or any lesser sea. Providence seems in a manner to invite us to the trial, as there are to our knowledge trading companies, whose commerce lies in many of the places where these barbarians dwell. At one time or other, ships are sent to visit places of more recent discovery, and to explore parts the most unknown. Every fresh account of their ignorance or cruelty should call forth our pity, and excite us to concur with providence in seeking their eternal good. Scripture likewise seems to point out this method. "Surely the isles shall wait for me, and the ships of Tarshish first, to bring thy sons from far, their silver and their gold with them, unto the name of the Lord thy God" (Isaiah 60:9). This seems to imply that in the time of the glorious increase of the church in the latter days (of which the whole chapter is undoubtedly a prophecy), commerce will serve as an instrument in the spread of the gospel. The ships of Tarshish were trading vessels which made voyages for traffic to various parts. Therefore, much must be meant by it, that navigation, especially that which is commercial, will be one great means of carrying on the work of God. And perhaps it implies that there will be a very considerable appropriation of wealth to that purpose.

Secondly—their uncivilized and barbarous way of living. This can be no objection to any except those whose love of ease renders them unwilling to expose themselves to inconveniences for the good of others. It was no objection to the apostles and their successors, who went among the barbarous Germans and Gauls, and still more barbarous Britons! They did not wait for the ancient inhabitants of these countries to be civilized before they could be Christianized, but went simply with the doctrine of the Cross.

Tertullian could boast that "those parts of Britain which were proof against the Roman armies were conquered by the gospel of Christ." It was no objection to an Elliot or a Brainerd, in later times. They went forth and encountered difficulties of every kind, and found that a cordial reception of the gospel produced those happy effects which the longest interactions with Europeans could never accomplish without the gospel. It is no objection to commercial men. It only requires that we should have as much love for the souls of our fellow creatures and fellow-sinners as they have for the profits arising from a few beaver skins, and all these difficulties would be easily surmounted.

After all, the uncivilized state of the heathen, instead of affording an objection *against* preaching the gospel to them, ought to furnish an argument *for* it. Can we as men, or as Christians, hear that ignorance and barbarism envelopes a great part of our fellow creatures—whose souls are as immortal as ours, and who are as capable as ourselves of adorning the gospel, and contributing by their preaching, writings, or practices, to the glory of our Redeemer's name, and the good of His Church? Can we hear that they are without the gospel, without government, without laws, and without arts and sciences, and not exert ourselves to introduce among them the sentiments of men, and of Christians? Would not the spread of the gospel be the most effectual means of their civilization? Would that not make them useful members of society?

We know that such effects did in a measure follow the a fore-mentioned efforts of Elliot, Brainerd, and others among the American Indians. And if similar attempts were made in other parts of the world, and were accompanied by a divine blessing (which we have every reason to think they would) might we not expect to see effective ministers, or clearly written defenses of the truth, even among those who at present seem to be scarcely human?

Thirdly—the danger of being killed by them. It is true that whoever does go must put his life in his hand, and not consult with flesh and blood. But doesn't the goodness of the cause, the duties incumbent on us as the creatures of God and as Christians, and the perishing state of our fellow men, loudly call upon us to venture all and use every warrantable exertion for their benefit? Paul and Barnabas, who "hazarded their lives for the name of our Lord Jesus Christ" (Acts 15:26) were not blamed as being rash but commended for so doing; while John Mark, who through timidity of mind deserted them in their perilous undertaking, was branded with censure. After all, as has been already observed, I greatly question whether most of the barbarities practiced by the savages upon those who have visited them have not originated in some real or supposed affront, and were therefore more properly acts of self-defense than proofs of ferocious dispositions. No wonder if the imprudence of sailors should prompt them to offend the simple savage, and the offense be resented.

But Elliot, Brainerd, and the Moravian missionaries have seldom been molested. Rather, the heathen have shown a general willingness to hear the Word; and have principally expressed their hatred of Christianity on account of the vices of nominal Christians.

Fourthly—the difficulty of procuring the necessities of life. This would not be so great as may appear at first sight. For though we could not procure European food, we could acquire the same food as the natives of those countries which we visit. And this would only be passing through what we have virtually engaged in by entering on the ministerial office. A Christian minister is not his own (1 Cor. 6:19); he is the *servant* of

God, and therefore ought to be wholly devoted to Him. By entering that sacred office, he solemnly undertakes to always be engaged as much as possible in the Lord's work, and not to choose his own pleasure or employment, or pursue the ministry as something subservient to his own ends or interests, or as a kind of bye-work. He engages to go where God pleases, and to do or endure what He sees fit to command or call him to in the exercise of his function. He virtually bids farewell to friends, pleasures, and comforts, and stands in readiness to endure the greatest sufferings in the work of his Lord and Master.

It is inconsistent for ministers to please themselves with thoughts of a numerous congregation, cordial friends, a civilized country, legal protection, affluence, splendor, or even sufficient income. The slights and hatred of men and even pretended friends, gloomy prisons and tortures, the society of barbarians of uncouth speech, miserable accommodations in wretched wildernesses, hunger and thirst, nakedness, weariness, hard work, and but little worldly encouragement, should rather be the objects of their expectation. This is how the apostles acted in the early days of Christianity. They endured hardness as good soldiers of Jesus Christ.

Although we are not called to suffer these things while living in a civilized country where Christianity is protected by law, I question whether all are justified in staying here while so many are perishing without means of grace in other lands. I am sure that it is entirely contrary to the spirit of the gospel for its ministers to share it from self-interested motives, or with great worldly expectations. On the contrary, the commission is a sufficient call to them to venture all, and like the early Christians, go everywhere preaching the gospel.

It might be necessary, however, for at least two to go together, and in general I should think it best that they should be married men. To prevent their time from being used to procure necessities, two or more other people, along with their wives and families, might also accompany them—wholly employed in providing for them. In most countries it would be necessary for them to cultivate a little spot of ground just for their support, which would be a resource to them whenever their supplies ran out. Not to mention the advantages they would reap from each other's company. It would take off the enormous expense which has always attended undertakings of this kind, the first expense being the whole. While a large colony needs support for a considerable time, so small a number would maintain themselves upon receiving the first crop. They would have the advantage of choosing their situation, and their wants would be few. The women, and even the children, would be necessary for domestic purposes. A few articles of stock (as a cow or two, a bull, and a few other cattle of both sexes), a few utensils of husbandry, and some corn to sow their land would be sufficient.

Those who attend the missionaries should understand husbandry, fishing, fowling, etc., and be provided with the necessary implements for these purposes. Indeed a variety of methods may be thought of, and once the work is undertaken, many things will suggest themselves to us—of which we have no idea at present.

Fifthly—learning their languages. The same means would be found necessary here as in trade between different nations. In some cases interpreters might need to be obtained and employed for a time. In places where these are not found, the missionaries must have patience, and mingle with the people till they have learned enough of the language to communicate their ideas to them. It is well known that no extraordinary talent is required to learn the language of any people on Earth in the space of a year or two, at most. At least enough of the language can be learned to convey any thoughts we wish them to understand.

The missionaries must be men of great virtue, prudence, courage, and patience; with established and unquestionable beliefs, and must enter with all their hearts into the spirit of their mission. They must be willing to leave all the comforts of life behind them, and to encounter all the hardships of a torrid or a frigid climate, an uncomfortable manner of living, and every other inconvenience that can attend this kind of undertaking. Clothing, a few knives, powder and shot, fishing tackle, and the articles of husbandry previously mentioned, must be provided for them.

When they arrive at the destination, their first business must be to gain some acquaintance with the language of the natives (for which purpose two would be better than one). By all lawful means, they must endeavor to cultivate a friendship, and to let them know as soon as possible the errand for which they were sent. The missionaries must endeavor to convince them that it was their good alone that induced them to forsake their friends and all the comforts of their native country. They must be very careful not to resent any injuries obtained, nor to think highly of themselves so as to despise the poor heathens—which might lay a foundation for their resentment, or rejection of the gospel. They must take every opportunity of doing them good.

Laboring and traveling night and day, they must instruct, exhort, and rebuke, with all long-suffering and eager desire for their welfare. And above all, they must be instant in prayer for the outpouring of the Holy Spirit upon the people of their charge. Let but missionaries of the above description engage in the work, and we will see that it is not impracticable.

It might likewise be important—if God should bless their labors—for the missionaries to encourage any appearance of gifts among the people of their charge. If such should be raised up, many advantages would be derived from their knowledge of the language and customs of their countrymen; and their change of conduct would give great weight to their ministrations.

Section 5

An enquiry into the duty of Christians in general, and what means ought to be used in order to promote this work.

If the prophecies concerning the increase of Christ's kingdom are true, and if what has been presented concerning His commission being obligatory on us is just, then it must be inferred that all Christians should heartily concur with God in promoting His glorious designs. For "...he that is joined unto the Lord is one spirit" (1 Cor. 6:17).

One of the first and most important of those duties incumbent upon us is "fervent and united prayer." Even though many may disregard and reject the influence of the Holy Spirit, all means which we can use will be ineffectual without prayer. If a temple is raised for God in the heathen world, it will not be "by might, nor by power," nor by the authority of the magistrate, or the eloquence of the orator; "but by my spirit, saith the Lord of hosts" (Zech. 4:6). Therefore, we must supplicate His blessing upon our labors in real earnest.

It is represented in the prophets that when there is "a great mourning in the land, as the mourning of Hadadrimmon in the valley of Megiddon, and every family shall mourn apart, and their wives apart," it shall all follow upon "a spirit of grace and supplication." And when these things shall take place, it is promised that "there shall be a fountain opened for the house of David, and for the inhabitants of Jerusalem, for sin, and for uncleanness, and that the idols shall be destroyed, and the false prophets ashamed" of their profession (Zech. 12:10–13:4). This prophecy seems to teach that when there is universal and fervent prayer, and all esteem Zion's welfare as their own, then numerous influences of the Spirit will be shed upon the churches; and will cleanse the servants of the Lord like a purifying fountain. This cleansing influence will not stop here. All old idolatrous prejudices will be rooted out, and truth prevail so gloriously that false teachers will be ashamed; so much so that they would rather be classed with obscure herdsmen, or the meanest peasants, than bear the humiliation associated with their defection.

The most glorious works of grace that have ever taken place have been in answer to prayer. It is in this way, we have the greatest reason to suppose that the glorious outpouring of the Spirit, which we expect at last, will be bestowed.

With respect to our own immediate connections, we have within these few years been favored with some tokens for good—granted in answer to prayer—which should encourage us to persist, and increase in that important duty. I trust our monthly prayer meetings for the success of the gospel have not been in vain. It is true that a lack of urgency generally attends our prayers. Yet feeble as they have been, it is believed that God has heard, and in a measure answered them. Evidently, the churches that have engaged in the practice have generally been on the increase since that time. Some controversies which have long perplexed and divided the church are stated more clearly than ever. There are calls to preach the gospel in many places where it has not usually been published. Yes, a glorious door has opened, and is likely to open wider and wider by the spread of civil and religious liberty, accompanied by a diminution of the spirit of Roman Catholicism.

A noble effort has been made to abolish the inhuman slave trade; though at present it has not been as successful as might be wished. Yet it is hoped that this fight will be persevered in till it is accomplished. In the meantime, it is satisfying to know that the recent defeat of the abolition of the slave trade has given the opportunity to introduce a free settlement, at Sierra Leone on the coast of Africa. This praiseworthy effort, if followed by a divine blessing, not only promises to open a way for honorable commerce with that extensive country and the civilization of its inhabitants; but may prove to be the happy means of introducing the gospel of our Lord Jesus Christ among them.

These are events that ought not to be overlooked or to be reckoned as small things. Yet, perhaps they *are* small compared with what might have been expected if all had cordially entered into the spirit of the proposal, so as to have made the cause of Christ their own. In other words, to have been as attentive to it as if their own advantage depended upon its success. If a holy solicitude had prevailed in all the assemblies of Christians on behalf of their Redeemer's kingdom, we might probably have seen before now not only an open door for the gospel (2 Cor. 2:12), but many "running to and fro, and knowledge...increased" (Dan. 12:4); or a diligent use of those means which providence has put in our power, accompanied with a greater than ordinary blessing from Heaven.

Many can do nothing but pray, and prayer is perhaps the only thing in which Christians of all denominations can cordially and unreservedly unite. But in this we may all be one, and in this the strictest unanimity ought to prevail. Were the whole body animated by one soul in this manner, then Christians would attend on all the duties of religion with great pleasure, and their ministers would attend on all the business of their calling with great delight. We must not, however, be content to pray without also putting forth the effort to obtain those things for which we pray. Were "the children of light" but as wise in their generation as "the children of this world" (Luke 16:8), they would stretch every nerve to gain so glorious a prize, nor ever imagine that it was to be obtained in any other way.

When a trading company obtains their charter, they usually go to its utmost limits. Their stocks, ships, officers, and men are so chosen and regulated as to be likely to answer their purpose; but they do not stop here. Encouraged by the prospect of success they use every effort, cast their bread upon the waters, cultivate friendship with everyone from whose information they expect the least advantage. They cross the widest and most tempestuous seas, and encounter the most unfavorable climates. They introduce themselves into the most barbarous nations, and sometimes undergo the most affecting hardships. Their minds continue in a state of anxiety and suspense, and a longer delay than usual in the arrival of their vessels agitates them with a thousand painful thoughts and foreboding apprehensions, which continue till the rich returns have safely arrived in port. But why these fears? What is the cause of all these concerns and why do they embark on this labor? Is it not because their souls enter into the spirit of the project, and in a way their happiness depends on its success?

Christians are a body whose truest interest lies in the exaltation of the Messiah's kingdom. Their charter is very extensive, their encouragements exceeding great, and the returns promised infinitely superior to all the gains of the most lucrative partnership. Let then everyone in his station consider himself as bound to act with all his might and in every possible way for God.

Suppose a company of serious Christians, ministers, and private individuals were to form themselves into a society, and make a number of rules respecting the regulation of the plan, and the people who are to be employed as missionaries, the means of defraying the expense, etc., etc. This society must consist of people whose hearts are in the work—men of serious religion, possessing a spirit of perseverance. There must be a determination not to admit any person who is not of this description, or to retain him longer than he answers to it.

From such a society a committee might be appointed, whose business it should be to procure all the information they could upon the subject, to receive contributions, to inquire into the characters, tempers, abilities, and religious views of the missionaries, and also to provide them with necessities for their undertaking.

They must also pay a great attention to the views of those who undertake this work; for want of this the missions to the Spice Islands sent by the Dutch East India Company were soon corrupted—many going more for the sake of settling in a place where temporal gain invited them than of preaching to the poor Indians. This soon introduced a number of indolent or profligate people, whose lives were a scandal to the doctrines which they preached. And because of them, the gospel was ejected from Ternate in 1694, and Christianity fell into great disrepute in other places.

If there is any reason for me to hope that I will have any influence on any of my brethren and fellow Christians, it will probably be among those of my own denomination. Therefore, I propose that such a society or committee be formed among the Particular Baptist denomination.

I do not mean by this in any way to confine it to one denomination of Christians. I wish with all my heart that everyone who loves our Lord Jesus Christ in sincerity would in some way or other engage in it. But in the present divided state of Christendom it would be more likely for good to be done by each denomination engaging separately in the work than if it were a combined effort. There is room enough for us all, without interfering with each other. If no unfriendly interference took place, each denomination would bear good will to the other, and wish and pray for its success, considering it as upon the whole friendly to the great cause of true religion. But if all were intermingled, it is likely their private discords might throw a damp upon their spirits, and much hinder their public usefulness.

In respect to contributions for defraying the expenses, money will doubtless be wanting. But suppose the rich were to invest a portion of the wealth over which God has made them stewards in this important undertaking. Perhaps there are few ways that would turn to a better account at last. This action should not be confined to the rich. If people in more moderate circumstances were to devote a portion of their annual increase to the Lord—suppose a tenth—it would not only correspond with the practice of the Israelites under the Mosaic economy, but of the patriarchs Abraham, Isaac, and Jacob, before that dispensation commenced. Many of our most eminent forefathers among the Puritans followed that practice. If that were but attended to now, there would not only be enough to support the ministry of the gospel at home, and to encourage village preaching in our respective neighborhoods, but to defray the expenses of carrying the gospel into the heathen world.

If congregations were to open subscriptions of one penny or more per week, according to their circumstances, and deposit it as a fund for the propagation of the gospel, much might be raised in this way. By such simple means they might soon have it in their power to introduce the preaching of the gospel into most of the villages in England. Although men are placed there, whose business it should be to give light to those who sit in darkness, it is well known that they do not have it. Where there was no person to open his house for the reception of the gospel, some other building might be procured for a small sum. And even then, something considerable might be spared for the Baptists, or other committees, for propagating the gospel among the heathen.

Many people have recently discontinued the use of West India sugar on account of the iniquitous manner in which it is obtained. Those families who have done so, and have not substituted anything else in its place, have not only cleansed their hands of blood, but have made a saving to their families—some of sixpence, and some of a shilling a week. If this or a part of this were appropriated to the uses previously mentioned, it would abundantly suffice. We have only to keep the end in view, and have our hearts thoroughly engaged in the pursuit of it, and means will not be very difficult.

We are exhorted to "lay up...treasure in heaven, where neither moth nor rust doth corrupt, and where thieves do not break through nor steal" (Matt. 6:20). It is also declared, that "whatsoever a man soweth, that shall he also reap" (Gal. 6:7). These Scriptures teach us that the enjoyments of the life to come bear a near relation to that which now is; a relation similar to that of the harvest and the seed.

While it is true that all the reward is of mere grace, it is nevertheless encouraging. What a treasure, what a harvest must await such characters as Paul, Elliott, Brainerd, and others who have given themselves wholly to the work of the Lord. What Heaven it will be to see the many myriads of poor heathens, of Britons among the rest, who by their labors have been brought to the knowledge of God. Surely a "crown of rejoicing" (1 Thess. 2:19) like this is worth aspiring to. Surely it is worthwhile to lay ourselves out with all our might in promoting the cause and the kingdom of Christ.

Original footnotes in 1818 edition.

[1]See Edwards on Prayer, on this subject, lately reprinted by Mr. Sutcliff.

²The account of this second journey into the heathen world is found in Acts 15:40–18:22.

³See Acts 18:23, and Gal. 1:2.

Afterword

William Carey's *An Enquiry* is an important book in the history of Bible-believing people. During the late 1700's, some Baptists in England had bunkered themselves away from sharing Jesus with their neighbors and with the world. They believed that the Great Commission—going to people, making disciples, baptizing and teaching them—was only for the apostles (Matt 28:19-20). Others in the denomination struggled with whether believing biblical doctrine was necessary to be a Christian, much less a Baptist.

William Carey's argument was logical—if the Great Commission was only for the apostles, then why do Christians still observe the ordinance of baptism? His conclusion, that the church is to seek the lost, reminded the Baptists of England and Bible-believing people today that the Great Commission is fundamental to the church's mission in the world.

In Carey's thinking, if one believes the Bible then he or she must share Jesus across the street and around the world. He believed that God's power enables this great undertaking. It is summed up in his famous phrase to, "expect great things from God and attempt great things for God!"

This is why Truett McConnell University exists. We are a liberal arts university built on the inerrancy and authority of the Bible. Our mission is to "equip students to fulfill the Great Commission by fostering a Christian worldview through a biblically-centered education in a family friendly environment."

Truett McConnell offers over 50 programs of graduate and undergraduate study. Every undergraduate major includes a Great Commission minor, with classes on the Bible, a history of the free church, theology, and missions.

We build our campus life and efforts around four pillars: Love the Lord, love His Word, love His church, and love the lost. We want every student to graduate with not just a career heading, but with a mission where they, as Carey put it, "expect great things from God and attempt great things for God."

If you have a question or interest in Truett McConnell University, we invite you to visit us at www.truett.edu or schedule a campus visit. We hope that this edition of *An Enquiry* fosters and/or reinforces your desire to seek out the lost.

Jesus said, "Follow Me and I will make you fishers of men" (Matthew 4:19; Mark 1:17). Let us follow Him faithfully, so that until He comes—we go!

Dave Eppling
Director of Presidential Projects
Truett McConnell University
2021

Addendum A: William Carey's Chart Analyzing World Population and Religious Belief at the End of the 18th Century

The following represents the full content drawn from Carey's chart in his original 1792 version of *An Inquiry* depicting estimates of world population and religious beliefs at the end of the 18th century. Rather than reproducing the somewhat confusing chart here, the editors chose to publish the chart's content in a more reader-friendly style in this section.

EUROPE[1]

    Great Britain: 680 miles in length, 300 miles in breadth; 12,000,000 inhabitants; Protestants of many denominations

    Ireland: 285 miles in length, 160 miles in breadth; 2,000,000 inhabitants; Protestants and Roman Catholics

    France: 600 miles in length, 500 miles in breadth; 24,000,000 inhabitants; Catholics, Deists, and Protestants

    Spain: 700 miles in length, 500 miles in breadth; 9,500,000 inhabitants; Roman Catholics

Portugal: 300 miles in length, 100 miles in breadth; 2,000,000 inhabitants; Roman Catholics

Sweden (including Sweden proper, Gothland, Shonen, Lapland, Bothnia, and Finland):800 miles in length, 500 miles in breadth; 3,500,000 inhabitants;The Swedes are serious Lutherans but most of the Laplanders are pagans and very superstitious.

Isle of Gothland: 80 miles in length, 23 miles in breadth; 5,000 inhabitants

Isle of Oesel: 45 miles in length, 24 miles in breadth;2,500 inhabitants

Isle of Oeland: 84 miles in length, 9 miles in breadth; 1,000 inhabitants

Isle of Dago: 26 miles in length, 23 miles in breadth;1,000 inhabitants

Isle of Aland: 24 miles in length, 20 miles in breadth;800 inhabitants

Isle of Hogland: 9 miles in length, 5 miles in breadth; 100 inhabitants

Denmark: 240 miles in length, 114 miles in breadth; 360,000 inhabitants; Lutherans of the Helvetic Confession

Isle of Zeeland: 60 miles in length, 60 miles in breadth; 284,000 inhabitants; Lutherans of the Helvetic Confession

Isle of Funen: 38 miles in length, 32 miles in breadth; 144,000 inhabitants; Lutherans of the Helvetic Confession

Isle of Arroe: 8 miles in length, 2 miles in breadth; 200 inhabitants; Lutherans of the Helvetic Confession

Isle of Iceland: 435 miles in length, 185 miles in breadth; 60,000 inhabitants; Lutherans of the Helvetic Confession

Isle of Langeland: 27 miles in length, 12 miles in breadth; 3,000 inhabitants; Lutherans of the Helvetic Confession

Isle of Laland: 38 miles in length, 30 miles in breadth; 148,000 inhabitants; Lutherans of the Helvetic Confession

Isle of Falster: 27 miles in length, 12 miles in breadth: 3,000 inhabitants; Lutherans of the Helvetic Confession

Isle of Mona: 14 miles in length, 5 miles in breadth; 600 inhabitants; Lutherans of the Helvetic Confession

Isle of Alsen: 15 miles in length, 6 miles in breadth; 600 inhabitants; Lutherans of the Helvetic Confession

Isle of Femeren: 13 miles in length, 8 miles in breadth; 1,000 inhabitants; Lutherans of the Helvetic Confession

Isle of Bornholm: 20 miles in length, 12 miles in breadth; 2,000 inhabitants; Lutherans

Greenland: Undiscovered; 7,000 inhabitants; Pagans and Moravian Christians

Norway: 750 miles in length, 170 miles in breadth; 724,000 inhabitants; Lutherans

24 Faro Isles: 4,500 inhabitants; Lutherans

Danish Lapland: 285 miles in length, 172 miles in breadth; 100,000 inhabitants; Lutherans and Pagans

Poland: 700 miles in length, 680 miles in breadth; 9,000,000 inhabitants; Roman Catholics, Lutherans, Calvinists, and Jews

Prussia:[2] 400 miles in length, 160 miles in breadth; 2,500,000 inhabitants; Calvinists, Catholics, and Lutherans

Sardinia: 135 miles in length, 57 miles in breadth; 600,000 inhabitants; Roman Catholics

Sicily: 180 miles in length, 92 miles in breadth; 1,000,000 inhabitants; Roman Catholics

Italy: 660 miles in length, 120 miles in breadth; 20,000,000 inhabitants; Roman Catholics

United Netherlands: 150 miles in length, 150 miles in breadth; 2,000,000 inhabitants; Protestants of several denominations

Austrian Netherlands: 200 miles in length, 200 miles in breadth; 2,500,000 inhabitants; Roman Catholics and Protestants

Switzerland: 260 miles in length, 100 miles in breadth; 2,880,000 inhabitants; Roman Catholics and Protestants

The Grisons: 100 miles in length, 62 miles in breadth; 800,000 inhabitants; Lutherans and Roman Catholics

The Abbacy of St. Gall: 24 miles in length, 10 miles in breadth; 50,000 inhabitants; Lutherans and Roman Catholics

Neufchatel: 32 miles in length, 20 miles in breadth; 100,000 inhabitants; Calvinists

Valais: 80 miles in length, 30 miles in breadth; 440,000 inhabitants; Roman Catholics

Piedmont: 140 miles in length, 98 miles in breadth; 900,000 inhabitants; Roman Catholics and Protestants

Savoy: 87 miles in length, 60 miles in breadth; 720,000 inhabitants; Roman Catholics and Protestants

Geneva, City: 24,000 inhabitants; Calvinist

Bohemia: 478 miles in length, 322 miles in breadth; 2,100,000 inhabitants; Roman Catholics and Moravians

Hungary: 300 miles in length, 200 miles in breadth; 2,500,000 inhabitants; Roman Catholics

Germany: 600 miles in length, 500 miles in breadth; 20,000,000 inhabitants; Roman Catholics and Protestants

Russia in Europe: 1,500 miles in length, 1,100 miles in breadth; 22,000,000 inhabitants; Greek Church

Turkey in Europe: 1,000 miles in length, 900 miles in breadth; 18,000,000 inhabitants; Greek Christians, Jews, and Muslims

Budziac Tartary: 300 miles in length, 60 miles in breadth; 1,200,000 inhabitants; Greek Christians, Jews, and Muslims

Lesser Tartary: 390 miles in length, 65 miles in breadth; 1,000,000 inhabitants; Greek Christians, Jews, and Muslims

Crim Tartary: 145 miles in length, 80 miles in breadth; 500,000 inhabitants; Greek Christians, Jews, and Muslims

Isle of Tenedos: 5 miles in length, 3 miles in breadth; 200 inhabitants; Muslims

Isle of Negropont: 90 miles in length, 25 miles in breadth; 25,000 inhabitants; Muslims

Isle of Lemnos: 25 miles in length, 25 miles in breadth; 4,000 inhabitants; Muslims

Isle of Paros: 36 miles in compass; 4,500 inhabitants; Greek Christians

Isle of Lesbos, or **Mitylene:** 160 miles in compass; 30,000 inhabitants; Muslims and Greeks

Isle of Naxia: 100 miles in compass; 8,000 inhabitants; Greeks and Roman Catholics

Isle of Scio, or **Chios:** 112 miles in compass; 113,000 inhabitants; Greek Christians, Roman Catholics, and Muslims

Isle of Nio: 40 miles in compass; 1,000 inhabitants; Greek Christians, Roman Catholics, and Muslims

Isle of Scyros: 60 miles in compass; 1,000 inhabitants; Greek Christians, Roman Catholics, and Muslims

Isle of Mycone: 36 miles in compass; 3,000 inhabitants; Roman Catholics and Muslims

Isle of Samos: 30 miles in length, 15 miles in breadth; 12,000 inhabitants; Muslims

Isle of Nicaria: 70 miles in compass; 3,000 inhabitants; Greek Christians

Isle of Andros: 120 miles in compass; 4,000 inhabitants; Greek Christians

Isle of Cyclades, Delos the Chief: 700 inhabitants; Greek Christians

Isle of Zia: 40 miles in compass; 8,000 inhabitants; Greek Christians

Isle of Cerigo, or **Cytheraea:** 50 miles in compass; 1,000 inhabitants; Greek Christians

Isle of Santorin: 36 miles in compass; 10,000 inhabitants; Greek Christians and Roman Catholics

Isle of Policandra: 8 miles in compass; 400 inhabitants; Greek Christians and Roman Catholics

Isle of Patmos: 18 miles in compass; 600 inhabitants; Greek Christians and Roman Catholics

Isle of Sephanto: 36 miles in compass; 5,000 inhabitants; Greeks

Isle of Claros: 40 miles in compass; 1,700 inhabitants; Muslims

Isle of Amorgo: 36 miles in compass; 4,000 inhabitants; Greek Christians

Isle of Leros: 18 miles in compass; 800 inhabitants; Christians and Muslims

Isle of Thermia: 40 miles in compass; 6,000 inhabitants; Greek Christians

Isle of Stampalia: 50 miles in compass; 3,000 inhabitants; Greek Christians

Isle of Salamis: 50 miles in compass; 1,000 inhabitants; Greek Christians

Isle of Scarpanta: 20 miles in compass; 2,000 inhabitants; Greek Christians

Isle of Cephalonia: 130 miles in compass; 50,000 inhabitants; Greek Christians

Isle of Zant: 50 miles in compass; 30,000 inhabitants; Greek Christians

Isle of Milo: 60 miles in compass; 40,000 inhabitants; Greek Christians

Isle of Corfu: 120 miles in compass; 60,000 inhabitants; Greek Christians

Isle of Candia, or **Crete:** 200 miles in length, 60 miles in breadth; 400,000 inhabitants; Greek Christians and Muslims

Isle of Coos, or **Stanchia:** 70 miles in compass; 12,800 inhabitants; Muslims and Christians

Isle of Rhodes: 60 miles in length, 25 miles in breadth; 120,000 inhabitants; Muslims and Christians

Isle of Cyprus: 150 miles in length, 70 miles in breadth; 300,000 inhabitants; Muslims

ASIA

Turkey in Asia (contains Anatolia, Syria, Palestine, Diabekr, Turcomania, and Georgia): 1,000 miles in length; 800 miles in breadth; 20,000,000 inhabitants; Muslims are most prevalent, but there are many Greek, Latin, Eutychian, and Armenian Christians

Arabia: 1,300 miles in length, 1,200 miles in breadth; 16,000,000 inhabitants; Muslims

Persia: 1,280 miles in length, 1,140 miles in breadth; 20,000,000 inhabitants; Muslims of the Sect of Ali

Great Tartary: 4,000 miles in length, 1,200 miles in breadth; 40,000,000 inhabitants; Muslims and Pagans

Siberia: 2,800 miles in length, 960 miles in breadth; 7,500,000 inhabitants; Greek Christians and Pagans

Samojedia: 2,000 miles in length, 370 miles in breadth; 1,900,000 inhabitants; Pagans

Kamtscatcha: 540 miles in length, 236 miles in breadth; 900,000 inhabitants; Pagans

Nova Zembla: Undiscovered; Thinly inhabited; Pagans

China: 1,400 miles in length, 1,260 miles in breadth; 60,000,000 inhabitants; Pagans

Japan (contains Niphon Island): 900 miles in length, 360 miles in breadth; 10,000,000 inhabitants; Pagans

Isle of Ximo: 210 miles in length, 200 miles in breadth; 3,000,000 inhabitants; Pagans

Isle of Xicoco: 117 miles in length, 104 miles in breadth; 1,800,000 inhabitants; Pagans

Isle of Tsussima: 39 miles in length, 34 miles in breadth; 40,000 inhabitants: Pagans

Isle of Iki: 20 miles in length, 17 miles in breadth; 6,000 inhabitants; Pagans

Isle of Kubitessima: 30 miles in length, 26 miles in breadth; 8,000 inhabitants; Pagans

Isle of Matounsa: 54 miles in length, 26 miles in breadth; 50,000 inhabitants; Pagans

Isle of Fastistia: 36 miles in length, 34 miles in breadth; 30,000 inhabitants; Pagans

Isle of Firando: 30 miles in length, 28 miles in breadth; 10,000 inhabitants; Pagans

Isle of Amacusa: 27 miles in length, 24 miles in breadth; 6,000 inhabitants; Pagans

Isle of Awasi: 30 miles in length, 18 miles in breadth; 5,000 inhabitants; Pagans

India (beyond the Ganges): 2,000 miles in length, 1,000 miles in breadth; 50,000,000 inhabitants; Muslims and Pagans

Indostan: 2,000 miles in length, 1,500 miles in breadth; 110,000,000 inhabitants; Muslims and Pagans

Tibet: 1,200 miles in length, 480 miles in breadth; 10,000,000 inhabitants; Pagans

Isle of Ceylon: 250 miles in length, 200 miles in breadth; 2,000,000 inhabitants; Pagans, except the Dutch Christians

Isle of Maldives: 1,000 in number; 100,000 inhabitants; Muslims

Isle of Sumatra: 1,000 miles in length, l00 miles in breadth; 2,100,000 inhabitants; Muslims and Pagans

Isle of Java: 580 miles in length, l00 miles in breadth; 2,700,000 inhabitants; Muslims and Pagans

Isle of Timor: 240 miles in length, 54 miles in breadth; 300,000 inhabitants; Muslims, pagans, and a few Christians

Isle of Borneo: 800 miles in length, 700 miles in breadth; 8,000,000 inhabitants; Muslims, pagans, and a few Christians

Isle of Celebes: 510 miles in length, 240 miles in breadth; 2,000,000 inhabitants; Muslims, pagans, and a few Christians

Isle of Boutam: 75 miles in length, 30 miles in breadth; 80,000 inhabitants; Muslims

Isle of Carpentyn: 30 miles in length, 3 miles in breadth; 2,000 inhabitants; Christian Protestants

Isle of Ourature: 18 miles in length, 6 miles in breadth; 3,000 inhabitants; Pagans

Isle of Pullo Lout: 60 miles in length, 36 miles in breadth; 10,000 inhabitants; Pagans

Besides the little Islands of Manaar, Aripen, Paradivia, Pengandiva, Analativa, Nainandiva, and Nindundiva, which are inhabited by Christian Protestants. And Banca, Madura, Bally, Lambeck, Flores, Solor, Leolana, Panterra, Miscomby, and several others inhabited by Pagans and Muslims.

The Moluccas are:

Banda: 20 miles in length, 10 miles in breadth; 6,000 inhabitants; Pagans and Muslims

Buro: 25 miles in length, 10 miles in breadth; 7,000 inhabitants; Pagans and Muslims

Amboyna: 25 miles in length, 10 miles in breadth; 7,500 inhabitants; Christians—the Dutch have 25 churches

Ceram: 210 miles in length, 45 miles in breadth; 250,000 inhabitants; Pagans and Muslims

Gillola: 190 miles in length, 110 miles in breadth; 650,000 inhabitants; Pagans and Muslims

And Pullo-way, Pullo-rin, Nera, Guamanapi, Guilliaien, Ternate, Motir, Machian, and Bachian, which are inhabited by Pagans and Muslims.

The Philippine Islands are supposed to be about 11,000; some of the chief are:

> **Isle of Mindanao:** 60 miles in length, 40 miles in breadth; 18,000 inhabitants; Pagans and Muslims
>
> **Isle of Bahol:** 24 miles in length, 12 miles in breadth; 6,000 inhabitants; Pagans and Muslims
>
> **Isle of Layta:** 48 miles in length, 27 miles in breadth; 10,000 inhabitants; Pagans and Muslims
>
> **Isle of Parragon:** 240 miles in length, 60 miles in breadth; 100,000 inhabitants; Pagans and Muslims

The Calamines are:

> **Sebu:** 60 miles in length, 24 miles in breadth; 10,000 inhabitants; Roman Catholics
>
> **Mindora:** 60 miles in length, 36 miles in breadth; 12,000 inhabitants; Pagans and Muslims
>
> **Philippina:** 185 miles in length, 120 miles in breadth; 104,000 inhabitants; Pagans and Muslims
>
> **Negroes Isle:** 150 miles in length, 60 miles in breadth; 80,000 inhabitants; Roman Catholics
>
> **Manilla:** 31,000 inhabitants; Roman Catholics and Pagans;
> The Ladrone Islands are inhabited by most uncivilized Pagans
>
> **New Holland:** 2,500 miles in length, 2,000 miles in breadth; 12,000,000 inhabitants; Pagans—one or two ministers are there
>
> **New Zealand** (two islands): 960 miles in length, 180 miles in breadth; 1,120,000 inhabitants; Pagans
>
> **New Guinea:** 1,000 miles in length, 360 miles in breadth; 1,900,000 inhabitants; Pagans
>
> **New Britain:** 180 miles in length, 120 miles in breadth; 900,000 inhabitants; Pagans
>
> **New Ireland:** 180 miles in length, 60 miles in breadth; 700,000 inhabitants; Pagans
>
> **Onrong Java:** A cluster of Isles; Pagans
>
> **New Caledonia:** 260 miles in length, 30 in breadth; 170,000 inhabitants; Pagans
>
> **New Hebrides:** Pagans;

Friendly Isles: 20 in number; Pagans

Sandwich Isles: 7 in number; 400,000 inhabitants; Pagans

Society Isles: 6 in number; 800,000 inhabitants; Pagans

Kurile Isles: 45 in number; 50,000 inhabitants; Pagans

Pelew Isles: Pagans

Oonalashaka Isle: 40 miles in length, 20 miles in breadth; 3,000 inhabitants; Pagans

The Other South Sea Islands: Pagans

AFRICA

Egypt: 600 miles in length, 250 miles in breadth; 2,200,000 inhabitants; Muslims and Jews

Nubia: 940 miles in length, 600 miles in breadth; 3,000,000 inhabitants; Muslims and Jews

Barbary: 1,800 miles in length, 500 miles in breadth; 3,500,000 inhabitants; Muslims, Jews, and Christians

Biledulgerid: 2,500 miles in length, 350 miles in breadth; 3,500,000 inhabitants; Muslims, Christians, and Jews

Zaara, or the **Desert:** 3,400 miles in length, 660 miles in breadth; 800,000 inhabitants; Muslims, Christians, and Jews

Abyssinia: 900 miles in length, 800 miles in breadth; 5,800,000 inhabitants; Armenian Christians

Abex: 540 miles in length, 130 miles in breadth; 1,600,000 inhabitants; Christians and Pagans

Negroland: 2,200 miles in length, 840 miles in breadth; 18,000,000 inhabitants; Pagans

Loango: 410 miles in length, 300 miles in breadth; 1,500,000 inhabitants; Pagans

Congo: 540 miles in length, 220 miles in breadth; 2,000,000 inhabitants; Pagans

Angola: 360 miles in length, 250 miles in breadth; 1,400,000 inhabitants; Pagans

Benguela: 430 miles in length, 180 miles in breadth; 1,600,000 inhabitants; Pagans

Mataman: 450 miles in length, 240 miles in breadth; 1,500,000 inhabitants; Pagans

Ajan: 900 miles in length, 300 miles in breadth; 2,500,000 inhabitants; Pagans

Zanguebar: 1,400 miles in length, 350 miles in breadth; 3,000,000 inhabitants; Pagans

Monoemugi: 900 miles in length, 660 miles in breadth; 2,000,000 inhabitants; Pagans

Sofala: 480 miles in length, 300 miles in breadth; 1,000,000 inhabitants; Pagans

Terra de Natal: 600 miles in length, 350 miles in breadth; 2,000,000 inhabitants; Pagans

Caffraria, or the **Hottentots Country:** 708 miles in length, 660 miles in breadth; 2,000,000 inhabitants; Pagans, and a few Christians at the Cape

Isle of Madagascar: 1,000 miles in length, 220 miles in breadth; 2,000,000 inhabitants; Pagans and Muslims

Isle of St. Mary: 54 miles in length, 9 miles in breadth; 5,000 inhabitants; French Catholics

Isle of Mascarin: 39 miles in length, 30 miles in breadth; 17,000 inhabitants; French Catholics

Isle of St. Helena: 21 miles in compass; 1,000 inhabitants; English and French Christians

Isle of Annabon: 16 miles in length, 14 miles in breadth; 4,000 inhabitants; Portuguese Catholics

Isle of St. Thomas: 25 miles in length, 23 miles in breadth; 9,000 inhabitants; Pagans

Isle of Zocotora: 80 miles in length, 54 miles in breadth; 10,000 inhabitants; Muslims

Comora Isles: 5 in number; 5,000 inhabitants; Muslims

Isle of Mauritius: 150 miles in compass; 10,000 inhabitants; French Catholics

Isle of Bourbon: 90 miles in compass; 15,000 inhabitants; French Catholics

Isle of Madeiras: 3 in number; 10,000 inhabitants; Roman Catholics

Cape Verd Isles: 10 in number; 20,000 inhabitants; Roman Catholics

Isle of Canaries: 12 in number; 30,000 inhabitants; Roman Catholics

Isle of Azores: 9 in number; 100,000 inhabitants; Roman Catholics

Isle of Maltha: 15 miles in length, 8 miles in breadth; 1,200 inhabitants; Roman Catholics

AMERICA

Brazil: 2,900 miles in length, 900 miles in breadth; 14,000,000 inhabitants; Pagans and Roman Catholics

Paraguay: 1,140 miles in length, 460 miles in breadth; 10,000,000 inhabitants; Pagans

Chili: 1,200 miles in length, 500 miles in breadth; 2,000,000 inhabitants; Pagans and Roman Catholics

Peru: 1,800 miles in length, 600 miles in breadth; 10,000,000 inhabitants; Pagans and Roman Catholics

Country of the Amazons: 1,200 miles in length, 900 miles in breadth; 8,000,000 inhabitants; Pagans

Terra Firma: 1,400 miles in length, 700 miles in breadth; 10,000,000 inhabitants; Pagans and Roman Catholics

Guiana: 780 miles in length, 480 miles in breadth; 2,000,000 inhabitants; Pagans and Roman Catholics

Terra Magellanica: 1,400 miles in length, 460 miles in breadth; 9,000,000 inhabitants; Pagans

Old Mexico: 2,220 miles in length, 600 miles in breadth; 13,500,000 inhabitants; Pagans and Roman Catholics

New Mexico: 2,000 miles in length, 1,000 miles in breadth; 14,000,000 inhabitants; Pagans and Roman Catholics

The States of America: 1,000 miles in length, 600 miles in breadth; 3,700,000 inhabitants; Christians of various denominations

Terra de Labrador, Nova-Scotia, Louisiana, Canada, and all the country inland from Mexico to Hudson's Bay: 1,680 miles in length, 600 miles in breadth; 8,000,000 inhabitants; Christians of various denominations, but most of the North American Indians are Pagans. California and along the western coast to 70 degrees south latitude, and inland so far as to meet the above article:2,820 miles in length, 1,380 miles in breadth; 9,000,000 inhabitants; Pagans.

All to the North of 70 degrees are Unknown and Pagans.

Cape Breton: 400 miles in length, 110 in breadth; 20,000 inhabitants; Christians

Cape Newfoundland: 350 miles in length, 200 miles in breadth; 1,400 inhabitants; Protestants

Cape Cumberland's Isle: 780 miles in length, 300 miles in breadth; 10,000 inhabitants; Pagans

Cape Madre de Dios: 105 miles in length, 30 miles in breadth; 8,000 inhabitants; Pagans

Cape Terra del Fuego: 120 miles in length, 36 miles in breadth; 5,000 inhabitants; Pagans

All the Islands in the vicinity of Cape Horn are Pagans.

The Bermudas: 16 miles in length, 5 miles in breadth; 20,000 inhabitants; Half English and Half Slaves

The Little Antilles are:

Aruba: 5 miles in length, 3 miles in breadth; 200 inhabitants; Dutch and Pagan Negroes

Curassoa: 30 miles in length, 10 miles in breadth; 11,000 inhabitants; Dutch and Pagan Negroes

Bonaire: 10 miles in length, 3 miles in breadth; 300 inhabitants; Dutch and Pagan Negroes

Margaritta: 40 miles in length, 24 miles in breadth; 18,000 inhabitants; Spaniards and Pagan Negroes

St. Trinidad: 90 miles in length, 60 miles in breadth; 100,000 inhabitants; Spaniards and Pagan Negroes

The Bahamas are:

Bahama: 50 miles in length, 16 miles in breadth; 16,000 inhabitants; Pagans

Providence: 28 miles in length, 11 miles in breadth; 6,000 inhabitants; Pagans

Besides Eluthera, Harbour, Lucayonegua, Andross, Cigateo, Guanaliana, Yumeta, Samana, Yuma, Mayaguana, Ynagua, Caieos, and Triangula are Pagans.

The Antilles are:

Cuba: 700 miles in length, 60 miles in breadth; 1,000,000 inhabitants; Roman Catholics

Jamaica: 140 miles in length, 60 miles in breadth; 400,000 inhabitants; English and Pagan Negroes

St Domingo: 450 miles in length, 150 miles in breadth; 1,000,000 inhabitants; French, Spaniards, and Negroes

Porto Rico: 100 miles in length, 49 miles in breadth; 300,000 inhabitants; Spaniards and Negroes

Vache, or **Cows Island:** 18 miles in length, 2 miles in breadth; 1,000 inhabitants; Spaniards and Negroes

The Virgin Isles are 12 in number, of which Danes Island is the principal Protestants.

The Carribbees are:

St. Cruz: 30 miles in length, 10 miles in breadth; 13,500 inhabitants; Danish Protestants

Anguilla: 30 miles in length, 9 miles in breadth; 6,000 inhabitants; Protestants and Negroes

St. Martin: 21 miles in length, 12 miles in breadth; 7,500 inhabitants; Protestants and Negroes

St. Bartholomew: 6 miles in length, 4 miles in breadth; 720 inhabitants; Protestants and Negroes

Barbuda: 20 miles in length, 12 miles in breadth; 7,500 inhabitants; Protestants and Negroes

Saba: 5 miles in length, 4 miles in breadth; l,500 inhabitants; Protestants and Negroes

Guardulope: 45 miles in length, 38 miles in breadth; 50,000 inhabitants; Catholics and Pagan Negroes

Marigalante: 15 miles in length 12 miles in breadth; 5,400 inhabitants; Catholics and Pagan Negroes

Tobago: 32 miles in length, 9 miles in breadth; 2,400 inhabitants; Catholics and Pagan Negroes

Desiada: 12 miles in length, 6 miles in breadth; 1,500 inhabitants; Catholics and Pagan Negroes

Granada: 30 miles in length, 15 miles in breadth; 13,500 inhabitants; English and Pagan Negroes

St. Lucia: 23 miles in length, 12 miles in breadth; 5,000 inhabitants; English and Native Pagan Caribs

St. Eustatia: 6 miles in length, 4 miles in breadth; 5,000 Whites, 15,000 Negroes; Dutch, English, etc.

St. Christopher: 20 miles in length, 7 miles in breadth; 6,000 Whites, 36,000 Negroes; English

Nevis: 6 miles in length, 4 miles in breadth; 5,000 Whites, 10,000 Negroes; English

Antigua: 20 miles in length, 20 miles in breadth; 7,000 Whites, 30,000 Negroes; English

Montserrat: 6 miles in length, 6 miles in breadth; 5,000 Whites, 10,000 Negroes; English

Martinico: 60 miles in length, 30 miles in breadth; 20,000 Whites, 50,000 Negroes; French

St. Vincent's: 24 miles in length, 18 miles in breadth; 8,000 Whites, 5,000 Negroes; The 8,000 are Native Caribs

Barbadoes: 21 miles in length, 14 miles in breadth; 30,000 Whites, 100,000 Negroes; English

Dominica: 28 miles in length, 13 miles in breadth; 40,000 Negroes; English, 2,000 of them are Native Caribs

St. Thomas: 15 miles in compass; 8,000 Negroes; Danish Protestants

[1][Original footnote in the 1818 edition here and below]: The indulgence of the reader is called for here. This table was made by Mr. Carey with fewer helps than are now at hand. However, at present it is not so incorrect but the reader may form a tolerably accurate idea of the state of the world. The impression made on the heathen world since 1790, when this scale was made, is glorious, but not so extensive as materially to involve the scale. We prefer its remaining as when first made.

[2]The rest of Prussian dominions being scattered about in several countries, are counted to those countries where they lie.

Contributors

Paige Patterson is a global theological educator with 60 years of ministry experience. He served as president of three theological institutions and as president of the Southern Baptist Convention. During the past six decades, Patterson has served as a member of many boards and councils including the International Council for Biblical Inerrancy. A native Texan, Patterson has served as pastor of churches in the United States in addition to his international ministry as a preacher and teacher at Bible conferences around the world. Dr. Patterson presently serves as President of The Sandy Creek Foundation (https://www.sandycreekfoundation.org).

Lea Eppling is a Christian author, editor, and presently serves as Ministry Coordinator at Bucky Kennedy Ministries, Gainesville, Georgia.

David Eppling presently serves as Director of Presidential Projects at Truett McConnell University in Cleveland, Georgia. He is a graduate of Luther Rice College (BA) and Southeastern Baptist Theological Seminary (MDiv, ThM).

www.ingramcontent.com/pod-product-compliance
Lightning Source LLC
Chambersburg PA
CBHW021450070526
44577CB00002B/340